# KUBERNETES

*A Step-by-Step Guide to Learn
and Master Kubernetes*

BRAYDEN SMITH

# TABLE OF CONTENTS

# Introduction

I want to thank you and congratulate you for purchasing *Kubernetes: A Step-by-Step Guide to Learn and Master Kubernetes*. This book contains proven steps and strategies on how to effectively use Kubernetes for various purposes.

The steps, examples, practical methods, and host of background information provide readers with strategies to operate Kubernetes in the most effective manner possible. Given that the nature of the Kubernetes platform is expansive and intricate, there is a conspicuous lack of text available to readers striving to acquire more information about the platform. Finally, this has changed.

With this text, all of the seemingly complicated and intricate facets of Kubernetes is presented in clear, informative detail that will facilitate a greater understanding of the platform as a whole. Also, each chapter is carefully constructed so that readers of all levels of familiarity with the platform are able to comprehend and appreciate the information therein. Given the rather complicated nature of the Kubernetes platform, it is in the best interest of users across all levels of familiarity and ability to learn the methods and strategies presented within this text.

One of the most beneficial aspects of this text is the problem-solving keys that are presented. Indeed, readers will acquire extensive knowledge about how to fix any of the most prevalent and persistent problems that are encountered when operating the Kubernetes platform.

The text starts off by presenting the various ways that Kubernetes operates, including how to maximize the functionality and performance of the platform. From there, deployment, pods, and services are presented in sequence with detailed information about configuration and other facets of the areas of Kubernetes. Thereafter, the chapters contain in-depth knowledge about Kubernetes extensions, Client Libraries, and Design Patterns.

Infused with the full expanse of modern, state-of-the-art information pertaining to the entire Kubernetes platform, readers will enjoy a pronounced advantage when operating it for various purposes and projects.

Thanks again for purchasing this book. I hope you enjoy it!

# Chapter 1

# How Kubernetes Operates

As a portable open-source platform that is also extensible, Kubernetes is excellent for effective management of multiple workloads and services that are containerized. In addition, Kubernetes allows for automation, along with declarative configuration, through its platform.

While Kubernetes offers many different and useful features across its platform, it can be thought of in three different ways:

1) Platform with micro-services

2) Container platform

3) Portable cloud platform

Notably, Kubernetes offers a management environment that is container-centric. In this way, Kubernetes manages networking and computing capabilities, as well as an extensive infrastructure for storage for user-friendly workloads. As a result, Kubernetes allows for the simplistic capability of a Platform as a Service (PaaS), along with Infrastructure as a Service (IaaS). What's more, Kubernetes facilitates increased portability among providers.

While Kubernetes enhances performance and functionality, there remain many situations that benefit from newer features. For instance, workflows that are specific to applications are able to be streamlined in order to augment the velocity of the developer. Impromptu orchestration usually needs intricate automation. This is the reasoning for Kubernetes being developed to be a platform that builds an arena of components and tools that ameliorate the process of scaling, deploying, and managing several different programs.

Moreover, labels give users the ability to organize and optimize resources in whatever manner they desire. Also, additions let users embed different resources with custom information. This allows users to more easily facilitate each workflow and enable a simpler method for tools of management to checkpoint state. It is also important to consider that the Kubernetes plane of control is developed on the exact same APIs that remain accessible to users. Not to mention, users are also able to write and develop their own controllers, including schedules, with the same APIs that can also be targeted by a command-line application.

In addition to detailing the sprawling benefits and features offered by Kubernetes, it is also equally important and beneficial to present and consider what Kubernetes does *not* offer users. For example, Kubernetes *cannot* be categorized as a traditional PaaS platform that is all-inclusive. As Kubernetes is an application that is operated at a container level, as opposed to hardware, Kubernetes gives features that are aligned with PaaS systems. These include deployment, logging, and scaling, to name a few. Nonetheless, Kubernetes is not inflexible—therefore, solutions that are "default" are thereby optional. Not to mention, Kubernetes gives solid foundational tools for creating different developer platforms—however, it sustains flexibility in important areas.

While not restricting the many forms of applications that it supports, Kubernetes is designed to support a multitude of workloads that are diverse. These include stateful, stateless, as well as workloads that are designed for processing complex data. Additionally, Kubernetes is an excellent choice for applications that run in containers.

Kubernetes is capable of source code deployment and will not allow users to put together their own unique applications. However, it will not provide users with services that are application-level, such as data processing frameworks, for example. These features can be operated on Kubernetes or are able to be accessed by applications operating through Kubernetes using portable features. Open Service Broker is an example one of these mechanisms that Kubernetes can be operated on.

It is also important to note that Kubernetes is not useful for alerting, dictating or monitoring solutions. Instead, Kubernetes facilitates any integrations in a manner consistent with proof of concept, along with many ways to collect and even export different metrics. Not to mention, Kubernetes is also insufficient for mandating and facilitating configuration systems and languages. Rather, Kubernetes will offer declarative API that could very likely be used for arbitrary systems and declarative specification.

If you are attempting to adopt a machine configuration that is relatively comprehensive or to use a platform for maintenance and self-healing systems, you will find that Kubernetes is not helpful for these purposes either. In addition, Kubernetes is not an orchestration system. Indeed, Kubernetes will eliminate orchestration altogether. Given that the technical and working definition for orchestration is executing an organized and designed workflow, Kubernetes is made up of a combined set of comparable and independent systems that continue to push a system's current state closer to the state that is desired.

Granted, it should not matter too much how you move through steps A to C; in other words, centralized control is not needed when using Kubernetes. As a result, you will end up with a system that is much easier to implement, and it will also be more powerful.

While it may certainly seem like there are many limitations in the way that Kubernetes operates, keep in mind that Kubernetes eliminates many formerly mandatory operation approaches, such as orchestration which requires that steps be executed following an "A to C" framework. In this way, Kubernetes expedites the process through which processes are executed, saving you time and effort.

So, why should you even consider using containers? The traditional method of deploying application systems was through installing applications onto a host that is using the operating system's package. As a result, this carried the unique advantage of entwining many different aspects such as libraries, executables, and life cycles with one another along with the OS host. In this traditional approach, users were able to construct virtual machine images to acquire rollbacks and rollouts. However, virtual-machine images are not portable and are heavyweight.

In the modern approaches, containers are deployed through operating-system virtualization as opposed to hardware. Notably, modern containers are separates from the host as well as one another. In this way, these modern containers have filesystems that are unique to them, are unable to view the processes of other filesystems, and, lastly, the computational resource of the new containers are able to be effectively bounded.

Also, new containers are far easier to construct than virtual-machines and are more portable along OS systems and clouds due to being decoupled from underlying infrastructure as well as the host filesystem. As most containers are relatively small in stature and operate at a fast rate, every container image can contain its own application within it. As a result, this relationship between the container image and application will unlock the full potential of containers. Through containers, immutable images in containers are able to be developed at a release/build time as opposed to deployment rate of time, because each of these applications is not required to be put together using the entirety of the application stack, and it does not need to be tethered to the overall infrastructure environment.

Producing container images in build and release time allows for an environment that is far more consistent and that can be carried from each stage to the next, such as from development to production, for instance. In the same way, containers are much more transparent when compared to virtual-machines—this allows for management and closer monitoring. What's more, this is even truer when considering that the container's lifecycle is managed specifically by the infrastructure instead of hiding from within the container by a process supervisor.

Lastly, with only a single application for each container, managing each container is analogous to managing the specific deploying of each application. We will examine the deployment of Kubernetes in more depth in Chapter 2.

From a general standpoint, Kubernetes can be seen as allowing for new patterns of design, much like design patterns that are object-oriented but for applications that are containerized. Indeed, the emergence of design patterns from within containerized architectures is not the least shocking, as most containers do provide a lot of that benefits and upsides as many software objects with regard to packaging, reuse, and even abstraction.

Further, due to containers usually engaging with one another through HTTP and other formats that are broadly available, such as JSON, the unique upsides are able to be provided in a manner that is independent of language.

As Kubernetes persists with bringing over 10 years of experience with Borg to the community of open source networking, the aim of Kubernetes is facilitating applications that are "cloud-active," as well as ensuring that application operations and deployment reliable and at scale.

Moreover, Kubernetes' projects and dedication to documenting all of their ideas surrounding design patterns for services that are container-based, including Kubernetes' allowing of such patterns, is the initial step in this direction.

What's more, Kubernetes is committed to working alongside practitioner and academic groups and communities to codify and identify other patterns, with the intention of assisting containers with fulfilling the dedication of fostering more reliability and simplicity to the whole lifecycle of software- ranging from operation to deployment and development.

# Chapter 2

# Kubernetes Deployment

Kubernetes Deployment, as per the official documentation, involves the user "describing the desired state in a Deployment object, through which the Deployment controller changes the actual state to the desired one at a controlled rate."

Prior to examining how Deployments specifically operate, it is important to consider that Kubernetes is an object store that also has code that is specifically designed to interact with the objects. Moreover, every object that is stored has 3 components: specification, current status, and metadata. The user's role is to provide the metadata, along with a specification where the desired state of each object is thereby described. Kubernetes works to ensure that this desired state manifests.

With regard to deployments, Kubernetes deployments oversee services that are stateless and can run on your cluster, rather than StatefulSets, which tend to manage stateful services. The purpose of deployments is to ensure that sets of identical pods are kept running and are then upgraded in a manner that is controlled. This is to say that rolling updates are performed by default.

You should also note that "Replicas" in key names refers to the specific number of pods that are replicated, as opposed to the number of ReplicaSets. Also, consider the following with regard to Kubernetes deployments:

- **Replicas** are copied directly from the spec. In a brief interval, you can read a deployment specifically where spec.replicas are not congruent with status.replicas.

- **availableReplicas** refers to the number of pods that are readily prepared for some time (minReadySeconds). As a result, this will certainly assist with preventing flapping of state.

- **unavailableReplicas** refers to the overall number of pods that you should ensure are present, minus the number of pods that have yet to be produced.

- **updatedReplicas** are the overall number of pods that are reachable by this specific form of deployment, as long as they match the spec template.

- **readyReplicas** are the total pod numbers that can be reached from deployment all the way through each of the replicas.

Kubernetes employs Conditions in many different areas of its platform. These are all lists of condition objects. Keep in mind that the very minimal object will contain a status, type, and reason.

Once you are equipped with a Kubernetes cluster, you are then able to deploy all of the containerized applications along with it fully. In order to do this, you will have to formulate a configuration of Kubernetes Deployment. In addition, the Deployment will inform Kubernetes on how to produce and update different instances of the system. After you have finally produced a Deployment, the Kubernetes master will schedule each mentioned applications and systems onto Nodes within the cluster.

Thereafter, when these application and system instances are produced, a Kubernetes Deployment Controller will begin to monitor each of those instances. Moreover, if the Node hosting a particular instance is deleted, the Deployment controller will then replace it. This is important because it will provide a mechanism of self-healing that effectively addresses machine failure as well as maintenance.

Prior to pre-orchestration, scripts for installation tended to be used primarily for starting certain applications. However, they would not allow for effective recovery from machine failure. Through simultaneously and independently producing application instances and maintaining their operation along Nodes, Deployments with Kubernetes offers a very different approach to management of applications.

Interestingly, you are able to manage and even create a Deployment quite easily by utilizing the Kubernetes command line, which is referred to as Kubectl. Further, Kubectl makes use of the Kubernetes API to engage with clusters.

When you begin to produce a Deployment, you will be required to be specific with the container image that you choose to incorporate for your application as well as the overall number of replicas that you wish to run. Also, you can adjust this information afterword simply by updating Deployment.

Remember that Kubernetes will automate deployment, application scaling, and operations. However, the goal of Kubernetes does not only pertain to system management, but it is also designed to assist all developers as well. In other words, Kubernetes should ease the process through which distributed services and applications running within datacenter and cloud environments are written. In order to trigger this, Kubernetes makes two primary designations: Kubernetes will define an API for applications that are containerized to engage with the particular management platforms, along with defining a certain API for administrators so that they can perform particular actions for effective management.

While much of the work on defining an API for applications that are containerized to interact with management platforms are still in the process of being refined, there have been some key features that have stemmed from this process already:

- The Kubernetes mechanism of **Graceful Termination** offers containers an increased amount of time before it is terminated, this may be due to a maintenance node drain, or even an update that is occurring on a rolling basis, and or a multitude of other reasons. This will allow an application to be shut down more efficiently without any hindrances.

- **ConfigMap** lets applications read configuration directly from Kubernetes as opposed to employing flags that are command-line.

- **Readiness probes** ensure a configurable application HTTP endpoint, although other forms are also supported. This allows for determining whether the container in question is ready to be the recipient of traffic and whether it is even alive. Moreover, this specific function and response will determine if Kubernetes will restart the container and or decide to incorporate it within the pool of load balancing for its service.

Deployments stand for a distinct collection of identical and multiple Pods devoid of any unique identities. It is important to note that a Deployment operates many different replicas of certain applications. This also replaces, in an automatic manner, replaces all particular occurrences when using the platform or else it will not respond. As a result, Deployments make sure that at least one, but likely more, of the instances that you encounter with your application are made available to serve all requests from the user.

Now, Deployments employ a template for Pods. This contains a certain specification for Pods. Moreover, the Pod distinction will ultimately determine the manner in which every Pod appears. This includes certain applications that are to operate within containers, along with

14

which volumes the Pods are to mount. Once a Deployment's Pod template is altered or morphed in some particular way, brand new Pods will be produced in an automatic fashion, one at a time.

Now, deployments are perfectly tailored for applications that are stateless and that employ only ReadOnlyMany features and volumes that are tethered to various replicas but are far from being a good fit for workloads that utilize ReadWriteOnce volumes. On the other hand, for stateful applications utilizing ReadWriteOnce features, StatefulSets is the best feature to use. These sets are designed to unload clustered and stateful applications that preserve information and data to storage that is persistent. Compute Engine is an example of this.

Producing deployments can be achieved by utilizing a few different commands. To name just a few, these include: Kubectl create, Kubectl run, and Kubectl apply. One these are produced, the Deployment will make sure that the user's desired amount of Pods will operate effectively, without glitches, and are available everywhere.

Moreover, Deployment will immediately replace all Pods that reach failure or are removed from nodes.

Updating deployments can be achieved by making certain alterations to Deployment's Pod template feature. Enforcing certain changes to this feature field will immediately cause a rollout of an update. In a default manner, whenever a Deployment is triggered and whenever an update ensues, the Deployment will halt the Pods and then diminish the overall amount of Pods to zero. Thereafter, it will terminate and drain the Pods altogether. The Deployment will then utilize the updated Pod template to raise brand new Pods.

Old Pods will not be taken out of the system until there are a sufficient amount of newer Pods that are up and operating. New Pods will not be produced until enough of the older Pods have been taken out. If you wish to view which Pods, and in what order, are brought forth and then removed from the system, users can run certain functions that the platform will provide.

Deployments make sure that, at the very least, one less than the total number of desired replicas is operating. In this instance, only one Pod, at the most, will be unavailable.

Finally, the life cycle and status of Deployments is worth deeper consideration. Notably, Deployments will be found in one of 3 different states at any particular time: Failed, Completed or Progressing.

A Failed state demonstrates that the Deployment has found one or more problems inhibiting it from finishing tasks that it has been assigned. Granted, some of these causes will include permissions and or quotas that are not sufficient, along with runtime errors, limit ranges or image pull errors. A Next, a Completed state suggests that Deployment has effectively finished all tasks that it has been assigned. In addition, this state indicates that all of the Pods are operating with the latest variation and are currently available. Also, this state suggests that there are no old Pods that are up and running.

Lastly, a progressing state suggests that the Deployment is currently in the process of performing particular tasks, such as scaling Pods and or bringing them up to the fore.

If users wish to investigate further about the specific causes of a Deployment's failure, they can examine all of the messages within the field labeled status:conditions.

# Chapter 3

# Kubernetes Pods

A pod can be referred to as a group of one or more containers with a shared network or storage, along with a certain specification for ways to operate each of the said containers.

The contents of a pod tend to consistently be found, scheduled, and operated/run within a context that is shared. Moreover, a pod will model application-specific logical host—this means that it will contain at least one application container coupled together within a pre-container system. These pre-container systems are operated within the same virtual or physical machine—thus, they would also then be executed within the same logical host.

Despite Kubernetes supporting many more container operating times than compared to Docker, the latter system is the better-known runtime. Therefore, it is more helpful for our purposes to describe pods using Docker terms.

A kubernetes pod operates within a shared context. Also, it is a Linux namespaces collection, cgroups, as well as many additional facets of isolation. You may notice that these are the exact same things that will isolate a Docker container.

Inside of the context of a pod, individual applications will very likely apply more sub-isolations. In addition, containers inside of a pod share a port space along with an IP address. These can be found by each other using localhost. These can also be controlled and communicated through standard inter-process communications such as SystemV as well as shared memory through POSIX.

For different pods, containers will have unique IP addresses and will not be able to communicate via IPC unless a special configuration is present. Not to mention, these containers tend to communicate with one another through the IP addresses of pods.

In these pods, shared volumes will be accessible to many applications—these volumes are designed as belonging to a pod and can also be easily mounted onto the filesystem of each application. With regard to Docker constructs, each pod is specifically designed as being in one Docker container collection within shared volumes as well as namespaces. Similar to individual container applications, pods are not generally considered durable systems and entities.

If a node gives out, pods that are assigned to that node are thereby arranged to be deleted. Rather than each pod being rescheduled to a brand new node, it is replaced by another pod that is identical to it. The same name can be kept for the new pod; however, a new UID will be required.

When something, such as a volume, for example, has a similar lifespan as a pod, this means that it will continue to exist so long as the pod with the UID also exists. If, for whatever reason, the pod is deleted or removed, despite providing an exact auxiliary, your related volume, for instance, will be obliterated then produced brand new.

A pod diagram will contain a web server as well as a file-pulling feature that utilizes a volume for shared storage found between each container.

## Pod Motivation

Pods are a configuration of patterned and cooperating processes that form a unit of service that is cohesive. Moreover, these pods will simplify the management and the deployment of applications by offering a high-level abstraction that superseded the level offered by their constituent applications.

Remember that pods are always serving as units of deployment, replication, and horizontal scaling. In addition, there are a few features that are managed automatically for containers within a pod—these include resource sharing, co-location, shared fate, and dependency management.

Among pods' constituents, pods facilitate sharing of data as well as communication. The network namespace will also be shared among apps found within them—similar to the mechanism that governs Internet Protocol as well as port space. As a result, they are able to more easily find and communicate with each other when they are using localhost. Consequently, all pod applications are required to coordinate how they use ports.

Every pod has its own IP address within a flat shared space used for networking that is also equipped with full communication with physical computers, as well as all of the other pods across a network. Note that the hostname will be set to the name of the pod for the application containers that exist within the pod.

Along with defining the container applications that operate within each pod, pods also specify a shared set of volumes. Further, volumes allow for data to persist through all restarts of a container along with being shared among all of a pod's applications.

A helpful benefit of pods is that you can easily utilize them in hosting app stacks that are vertically integrated, whose fundamental goal lies in aiding co-managed as well as co-located systems, which then include:

-   cache managers, management systems for content, loaders for data and files

-   snapshotting, compression, and log and checkpoint backup

-   event publishers, data change watchers

Individual pods are not designed to operate instances simultaneously within a shared application.

So, you might be wondering why you can't just run multiple programs at the same time within a single container? (Docker container)

Well, there are 3 primary reasons. First, for easing the use of the application. This is to say that users do not necessarily need to operate their own process managers, along with worrying about certain propagation for exit codes and certain signals.

Also, for reasons of transparency, letting the containers that can be found inside the pods to be more present in the overall infrastructure allows process management as well as monitoring resources. Moreover, this allows more convenient operation for all users of the system.

Also, separating and or decoupling software dependencies is another reason. Individual containers are able to be redeployed, rebuilt and even versioned under certain conditions. In addition, Kubernetes might even allow for supporting live updates pertaining to individual containers. Lastly, efficiency is another why you cannot run multiple programs the exact same time in a single container, which is due to the fact that as the infrastructure attracts more responsibility, containers will also be lighter in weight.

## Lack of Durability in Pods?

Notably, pods are not typically intended to necessarily be used as entities that are more durable and long-lasting. This is because they will not be able to persist through failures pertaining to scheduling, along with evictions and node failures. For the record, other evictions include not having resources (or even node maintenance, for this particular instance). Generally speaking, people should refrain from producing pods directly. Instead, they should focus on using controllers for singletons, such as Deployments, for instance. The benefit of the controller is that they induce the redevelopment of oneself. Even more, controllers such as StatefulSet will provide additional effective support to pods that are stateful.

The effective usage of APIs, in terms of being your main customer-dealing primitive, proves to be quite typical with respect to other cluster arranging mechanisms.

Effective use of APIs (collective) as the main user-facing primitive is typical among many cluster scheduling systems.

Also, a kubernetes pod can be revealed as a primitive to ensure the following:

- Pod-level operations support (devoid of having to "proxy" through API controllers)

- Decoupling of lifetime pod from controller lifetime (this includes bootstrapping as well)

- Exposing the pod to facilitate "pluggability" of controller and scheduler

- Cluster-level functionality

Pods are the tiniest and most rudimentary of the deployable objects within the entire Kubernetes platform. Moreover, it signifies an instance of a running process that is occurring within a cluster that you are using.

Notably, Pods carry at least one or more containers within them. These often include Docker containers. Whenever a Pod operates a few containers at the same time, these containers will be managed as singular entities that are tethered to a Pod's resources. In most cases, operating multiple containers within a Pod is used only in advanced instances.

Users should consider Pods to be isolated and self-contained "logical hosts." These will carry systemic needs of whichever applications that it is assigned to serve. Moreover, a Pod's overall purpose is to operate only one instance of an application on a cluster. Nevertheless, users are not recommended to produce individualized Pods. Rather, they are well-advised to produce a collection of Pods that are identical to one another in order to run a particular application effectively.

What's more, replica Pods are overseen and produced by a specific *controller;* a Deployment is an example of a controller. The A in responsibility of controllers is to effectively manage and oversee lifespan of Pods, while also performing something called horizontal scaling. While one may consider having Pods be interacted with in order to inspect, troubleshoot or even debug, controllers are strongly recommended for managing a Pod.

Pods, running on nodes within a cluster, will remain tethered to the said node until the full expanse of the process has been completed.

Then, the Pod will be deleted and evicted from this node because of a lack of resources, or if the node fails. In the case of the latter, a Pod that is on the node will be immediately deleted.

## Terminating Pods

As pods tend to be more representative of running certain processes that are on nodes with the cluster, you should allow these particular processes to be terminated once they are not needed any longer, as opposed to being deleted while comprising of some kill signal as well as not being given the opportunity of cleaning up.

It is also important to note that users should be capable of requesting immediate deletion as well as knowing when processes are to be terminated. Also, users should also be capable of making sure that all of their deletes are completed and followed through with.

Whenever a certain user wants to delete a pod, the system will thereafter record whatever the intended grace period is prior to the pod being allowed to be killed off. In addition, this must occur before your containers' main processes receive the TERM signal.

Upon having a certain time elapses, these processes then receive your KILL signal, thus enabling your API server's pod to be obliterated. In case that you reignite your container (or what's referred to as Kubelet) when anticipating the processes' cancellation, this deletion process, as well as your grace period, is going to get stopped.

Below is an example of a flow:

1. The consumer directs a particular order of obliterating the Pod; the period of grace here is 30 seconds.

2. Within your API server, a Pod is continually renewing even upon surpassing the time that it is deemed to be dead.

3. Your Pod appears as to be Terminating when it is posted within client commands.

4. In conjunction with step #3, whenever the Kubelet views that a certain Pod is marked as having been terminated (or in the process), given that the duration pertaining to step #2 is already fixed, the process of terminating your Pod will then start.

5. If one of the Pod's containers has uniquely defined a preStop hook, it is then imprinted within a container. If, for instance, the particular preStop hook is continuing to operate once the grace period has ended, the 2nd step is then imprinted along with a relatively small grace period (extended by nearly 3 seconds).

6. Next, the container is delivered the TERM signal. Keep in mind that not every container within the Pod will automatically receive the TERM signal at the exact same moment and might even need a preStop hook if they must be shut down in a certain order.

7. In conjunction with step #3, Pod is to be immediately removed from each endpoint list for service, and will not be considered germane to the set of operating pods for replication controllers. It is important to note that the Pods that shutdown incrementally will not be able to serve traffic because load balancers will remove them from all of their locations.

8. While the grace period is no longer operating, any of the processes that are continuing to operate within the Pod end up being terminated using SIGKILL.

9. Finally, your Kubelet is eventually going to complete the deletion of your POD from your API server through establishing a zero grace period, which signifies instantaneous removal. Thereafter, your Pod is then nowhere to be found in your API or is already inaccessible to your client.

Another important note relating to pods is their force deletion. This can adequately refer to the pods' removal from your cluster state as well as etcd. Moreover, whenever this happens, your kubelet's approval is no longer necessitated by your apiserver.

This will then remove your pod right away in order to give way to a brand new one with a similar name. Those established to be deleted right away, particularly the ones on your node, will still be afforded a short period of grace prior to being force deleted.

Granted, users should note that this may prove harmful to many of your pods. Thus, caution is necessary when they are performed.

Pod containers also incorporate a privileged mode. As per Kubernetes version 1.1, this particular mode is activated through employing a pod's privileged flag right on your container spec's SecurityContext. Notably, it's especially helpful in getting containers to employ abilities aligned with Linux, such as manipulating the accessing devices and network stack.

Processes that are in the container tend to retrieve nearly the same privileges that ones that are external to the container also have. In the aforementioned mode, writing volume and network plugins are bound to be simpler as individual pods free from needing to be stacked within your kubelet.

# Chapter 4

# Kubernetes Services

A kubernetes service is generally considered a REST object. Indeed, this is very similar to a kubernetes pod. In the same way as all of the REST objects, a SERVICE is signified by having the ability to get included in your apiserver in order to produce an entirely new instance. Say, you have a set of PODs and that all of them expose your port 9376 then possess an "app=MyApp" label.

This particular specification is able to produce a brand new Service object that is labeled as "my-service" that will then target TCP port 9376 on any specific Pod that carries the label of "app=MyApp."

Notably, the said Service is then to be given a specific IP address, which is also referred to as "cluster IP." This is also used by Service proxies. Keep in mind that a Service is uniquely capable of mapping an incoming port to any targetPort in the system. In practice, your targetPort is to be given value identical to that of your port field.

Interestingly, the targetPort can refer to the same of a port in the backend Pods. In this way, the targetPort can be a string. The specific number that is thereafter assigned to that name does not have to be the same in each of the backend Pods.

Consequently, this will provide more deployment flexibility and will allow for Services to evolve. To exemplify, you are able to alter the number of the pros that each pod exposes in the subsequent version of your software backend. This can be done without having to break clients.

Take note that kubernetes Services are capable of supporting protocols for TCP, SCTP, and UDP. The default setting is TCP.

Services commonly abstract kubernetes Pods' access; however, they are also capable of abstracting other backend forms. For instance, you should aim to have a database cluster (external) during production; however, when testing, you should use databases that are your own. Also, you should strive to aim your service to a different service that can be found within another Namespace, or even within another cluster altogether.

It is important to note that because you're transferring all of the existing workloads to kubernetes, several backends will then operate externally to it. Now, considering this, you are able to define a certain service without also including a selector.

## Proxy-Mode

With regard to this mode, kube-proxy keeps watch over the Kubernetes master for the specific elimination of Endpoints as well as Service objects. This then enables access to a port that is selected randomly on your local node for each specific Service.

Note that any particular connections related to this port are to be proxied to one of the backend Pods of the Service—just as it is reported in Endpoints. Any backend Pod that is used will be determined in accordance with your SessionAffinity for each Service.

Finally, this will automatically install iptables rules designed to encapsulate all of the traffic to the Service's virtual cluster along with the Port and will redirect all of the traffic to the proxy port responsible for proxying the backend Pod. Notably, the selection of the backend is round-robin (this is done by default).

There are particular environmental variables for Kubernetes Services that should be considered as well. For example, whenever a Pod is operated on a Node, the kubelet will then add a stack of environment variables for every active Service in the system. Moreover, it will then support both of the Docker links.

Thankfully, this process will not require any order. Instead, any Service that a specific Pod is trying to acquire access to will have to be produced *prior* to the Pod itself. If not, the variables within the environment will be unpopulated. However, this restriction does not apply to DNS systems.

With regard to DNS systems, it is strongly recommended (though optional) add-on for a cluster is a DNS server. The DNS server will survey the Kubernetes API for all new Services and will then create a stack of DNS records for all of them as well. If, for instance, DNS is made accessible within your entire cluster, every single Pod will then have the capability of performing name resolution of all Services. on their own.

## Headless Services

On certain occasions, however, you will not be required to incorporate load-balancing and single service IPs. For the said instance, it is necessary to produce "headless" services by providing the destination "None" to your cluster IP.

The said option then facilitates all developers in limiting Kubernetes systems coupling by allowing more autonomy to perform discoverer on their own.

Applications will still be able to use a pattern of self-registration. Also, all other forms of discovery systems can be built rather easily on this specific API.

As such, for the said Services, a cluster IP will not be allocated as kube-proxy and will not handle any of these services for you—and the platform will not conduct proxying and load balancing.

The specific way in which DNS is configured will entirely hinge on if the service contains selectors that are defined.

For defined selectors, endpoints controller will create Endpoints records within the API. Also, they will modify the DNS configuration so that it returns A records pointing to Pods backing the Service.

Devoid of selectors, Endpoints controller will not produce records for Endpoints. Nonetheless, the DNS system will configure and search for the following:

CNAME records for ExternalName-type services.

## Publishing Services

Now, for certain aspects of the application that you are using, front ends are an example, you might wish to reveal a particular Service directly on an IP address that is external (located on the outside of a cluster).

Kubernetes ServiceTypes will enable greater specification of the exact type of service that you wish to retrieve. Remember that your preliminary setting is ClusterIP.

Type values, along with these values' specific behaviors, are the following:

**ClusterIP:** It reveals the service directly on an IP that is cluster-internal. This is significant because selecting this value will allow the service only to be accessible from inside of the cluster. Notably, ServiceType is the default.

**NodePort:** It reveals each Node's IP service at a port that is static. Also, a ClusterIP service that the NodePort service is designed to route to will be produced automatically. This will allow you to more easily contact the NodePort service externally from the cluster through the following request: <NodeIP>:<NodePort>.

**LoadBalancer:** It is responsible for exposing service in an external manner by employing a load balancer from a cloud provider. In this way, ClusterIP and NodePort are produced (the external load balancer will route to this).

**ExternalName:** It maps the specific service to each of the contents within the field of the externalName. It does this by returning, with its value, a CNAME record. Remember that no proxy is going to be set up in this scenario. A version of 1.7 or above of kube-dns will be needed.

The Kubernetes master is then going to automatically assign a port from a field determined through your ServiceNode; this is only in instances where you first establish the type field to NodePort. Thereafter, all of the Nodes will then proxy the port into the service that you are using- with the same port number on all of the Nodes. The port will be reported directly into your Services field.

If you wish to select certain IPs so that you can proxy your port, your nodeport-addresses kube-proxy flag should be set to specific blocks of IP. This has been supported since v1.10 Kubernetes.

To retrieve a particular port number, you are able to select a certain value in a nodePort field. Then, your chosen port is then going to be assigned to you by the system. If this path is not chosen, the API transaction will not succeed. Also, keep in mind that you are required to care for any collisions with the port on your own. Not to mention, the specific value that you select will have to be within a configured range for node ports.

Thankfully, it affords programmers their autonomy of establishing their respective load balancers and create environments not supported by Kubernetes in their entirety.

On providers of Cloud, which are responsible for supporting load balancers that are external, establishing the Type field to LoadBalancer will provide for your Service its own load balancer.

Producing the land balancer occurs in an unsynchronized manner, and all of the information therein pertaining to the balancer will be directly punished within the field. Moreover, all of the external load balances' traffic is then going to be directed to your backend Pods. The exact process in which this will operate will entirely depend upon whatever cloud provider is being used. Note that a considerable number of cloud providers do permit for loadBalancerIP to be given a specification.

For these instances, the load-balancer will be produced with the chosen loadBalancerIP. In case, however, that your loadBalancerIP isn't given a specification, another IP will be assigned to this loadBalancer (this new IP will be ephemeral). On the other hand, if the loadBalancerIP is given a certain specification, but the feature is unsupported by the cloud provider, the field will not be acknowledged.

For internal load balancing, it may be vital to direct all traffic from services existing within the same VPC that is being used. Note that this is primarily needed within a mixed environment. In contrast, within a DNS environment that is split-horizon, you will be required to utilize 2 specific services in order to route internal and external traffic toward your endpoints.

# Chapter 5

# Kubernetes Design Patterns

Following programming that had been object-oriented for many years, the emergence and documentation of design patterns occurred. Moreover, all of these patterns regularized and codified general problem-solving approaches to particular common programming issues that many systems faced. Furthermore, this codification process enhanced the general modernized programming due to making it much easier for programmers with less experience to create code relatively well-engineered. This then leads to the creation of reusable libraries and made codes far easier, faster, and more reliable to create.

The modern, or "state-of-the-art" with regards to distributed system engineering, has an appearance very similar to programming in the early 80s as opposed to development that is object-oriented.

Still, it's clear from viewing how successful MapReduce patterns have been with regards to bringing "Big Data" programs to the fore in many different developers and fields, that quality can be greatly improved by instilling effective patterns. Also, accessibility and speed can improve the quality as well in distributed system programming.

Nevertheless, the success that MapReduce has enjoyed is mostly limited only to. Single language for programming. Creating a fully comprehensive package of patterns for system designs will require simpler, and more generic vehicles that are language-neutral to convey all of the various atoms within the system.

As a result, it is fortunate that recent years have experienced a stark rise in Linux container technology being adopted. The container and image for the container are abstractions that are required for developing system patterns that are distributed.

Until this point, container images and containers have garnered most of their popularity through being more reliable and effective for delivering software through all of its stages, from development to production. By being continually sealed, with dependencies carries along with them, and thereby fostering deployment signals that are atomic, they will enhance the previous modern deploying software within the cloud or datacenter.

In this way, containers still carry potential to be more than merely a vehicle for deployment—they can also be similar to objects within software systems that are object-oriented.

Single-container management patterns offer a natural boundary for interface categorizing, analogous to the object boundary. Further, containers can reveal not only functionality that is application-specific, but hooks used for management systems as well. Granted, the traditional and most commonly used interface for container management is very, very limited. Generally, containers export 3 key verbs: stop, pause and run. While this interface is not entirely useless and does still have value, a richer more modernized and interface offers far greater utility to operators and developers of systems. With the broad support for HTTP web servers within most state-of-the-art programming language expansive support for many formats such as JSON, it can be relatively simple to define management API that is HTTP-based that is able to be implemented by ensuring that the container host a web server that certain end-points, along with its main function.

In this upward direction, the container is able to reveal a richer collection of information for applications, which incorporates including application-specific metrics for monitoring. Conversely, in the downward direction, the specific container interface will facilitate an environment to define and clarify lifecycles that ease writing components for software operated by management configurations and systems.

For instance, a management system for clusters will usually allocate certain priorities to particular assignments and tasks. However, tasks that are considered to be more important, or "higher priority" will be operated even in instances when clusters are oversubscribed. This is enforced by removing tasks that are less of a priority. Until resources are made available, these lower-priority tasks will have to wait.

Removing tasks of lesser priority, or evicting them, can be achieved through deleting the low-priority task. However, this will burden developers to more urgently respond to death that occurs in any area of the code.

In the instance of a lifecycle that is formal being defined between management and application system, the components of the applications will be able to be managed much easier because they conform to a contract that is more defined. Also, the system's development will be made easier because the developer is able to rely on the contract.

To exemplify, Kubernetes employs a deletion that is "graceful." This is a Docker feature that will immediately warn a container through the SIGTERM signal that it will be terminated. This warning provides a period of time that is application-defined prior to the SIGKILL signal being sent. As a result, this allows the application to be terminated in a cleaner manner through completing operations in-flight.

An example of a lifecycle that is more complex, think about the Android Activity model; it features many callbacks as well as a more defined machine state for the way that the system will trigger callbacks. Devoid of Android lifecycles that are formal and reliable, these lifecycles would be much more difficult to formulate.

Within container-based systems, this will mainly generalize to hooks that are application-defined and triggered once a container is produced, terminated and started.

Another form of Kubernetes design patterns is multi-container and single-node application patterns. Past the single container interface, many design patterns that span containers will begin to emerge. The patterns mentioned the far are examples of this. However, single node patterns are comprised of symbiotic containers co-scheduled directly not a single host machine.

Managing containers in system support for co-scheduling a few containers as one atomic unit—this is an abstraction that Kubernetes refers to as "Pods." On the other hand, Nomad calls this, "task groups." As a result, this is a required feature if you wish to facilitate patterns.

## Sidecar Patterns

This is broadly considered the most common pattern deployments for multi-containers. The role of sidecars is to improve and expand the system's main container. For instance, there may be a scenario where the main container could be a server on the web, and it may even be coupled with a "logsaver" sidecar that is responsible for collecting the web server's logs located in the local disk. Thereafter, it is streamed toward a cluster storage system.

Also, another example that occurs quite often is when a web server from disk content (local) that comes to be populated by a sidecar container. Further, this sidecar container will, once in a while, sync content from a repository and or another source of data.

Both examples presented here tend to be most common at Google. Indeed, sidecars are realized and made possible due to containers sharing a machine will also share a localized disk volume.

It is certainly possible to effectively construct the functionality of sidecars directly in the main container. Still, however, there remain several different benefits to employing separate containers.

Sidecar containers are still able to be configured in a manner that affords low-latency responses that remain consistent, especially with regard to low-latency queries. Nevertheless, this is only the case where the logsaver container is specifically configured for the purpose of scavenging extra cycles of CPU whenever the web server isn't too busy.

Also, the sidecar container is the particular unit of packaging; therefore, parting serving and log-saving into a multitude of containers will ease the division of responsibilities, thereby allowing for independent testing.

Additionally, sidecar containers are also the unit of reuse, so they can be coupled with various "main" category containers. Moreover, sidecar containers afford failure containment boundaries, thereby enabling the overall system to diminish in a relatively graceful manner.

Finally, the container is foundational the deployment unit; this allows for all of the various aspects of functionality to be improved/upgraded, as well as rolled back when it needs to be (independently). It is worth noting this benefit is accompanied by a drawback: the matrix setup for testing the system altogether needs to consider the entirety of the combinations for the container version that one may encounter in production. These can be relatively expansive because containers, on the whole, cannot be atomically upgraded.

It is granted that a monolith application will not have this same problem—still, systems that are componentized will be far easier to test in many different ways because they are constructed from smaller units that are able to be tested in an independent manner.

## Ambassador Patterns

Ambassador containers are able to proxy all communication to and from main containers. For instance, a developer may choose to couple a specific application that communicates to a protocol for memcache with a twemproxy ambassador. This is due to the application assuming that it is communicating on localhost to an individual memcache.

This specific category of container pattern is useful because it simplifies a programmer's processes in 3 distinct ways:

1. Programmers will only have to consider programming with regard to their application being connected to a localhost single server.

2. This allows them to test the application on its own through running a memcache on a machine that is local rather than an ambassador.

3. Programmers are able to recycle a twemproxy ambassador along with subsequent applications that may employ different language for coding.

Adapter patterns are the final single-node pattern—as opposed to the aforementioned ambassador pattern, which is responsible for presenting applications with a clarified and simple view of different applications. This is achieved through having output and interfaces be standardized along a multitude of different containers.

An established example of adapter patterns is that adapters make sure that containers within a given system share an interface for monitoring. Currently, applications employ a broad range of methods and strategies for exporting metrics. Still, it remains much easier for single monitoring tools to gather metrics from sets of applications that are heterogeneous as long as all applications in the system are equipped with a monitoring interface that is consistent.

With regards to Google, the code convention has already been achieved. However, this is possible only when building software from the ground up. Moreover, this adapter pattern allows for heterogeneous open-source applications to create an interface that is uniform devoid of having to modify original applications.

Notably, main containers are able to "speak" with adapters by using a shared local volume or localhost. Keep in mind that although many current saluting for monitoring is capable of communicating with different types of backends, they employ codes that are application-specific within the monitoring system. As a result, this affords to separate concerns in a manner that is not as clean.

Expanding ahead of containers that are cooperating within a single machine, modular containers ameliorate constructing coordinated applications that are multi-node and distributed.

Among the biggest and predominate issues within distributed systems are leader elections. Though replication can be utilized in a way that shares load with a multitude of similar instances of components, a more intricate employment of replication are applications that require having to distinguish a "leader" from a specific replica.

Other replicas are available to replace the leader in an expedited way if they experience failure. Also, a certain system might operate a collection of leader election in a parallel manner. This may be done in order to determine the leaders of a multitude of shards. In addition, there are many different libraries for triggering a leader election. Generally, these are very complicated to fully 'understand and employ effectively. They are also inhibited by having to be used with a certain language for programming.

Alternatively, attaching a leader election and its library to an application is to employ a container for a leader election. Further, a collection of leader-election containers is capable of triggering an election on their own. They are also able to present a more simplified version of HTTP API on localhost to an application that needs a leader election.

Leader-elect containers are capable of being built only once, only by programmers who are experienced in this department. Subsequent interfaces can be recycled by developers for applications without having considered the language of implementation.

## Work Queue Patterns

Work queues, in the same way as leader elections, are a thoroughly examined topic with a multitude of frameworks that implement them. Also, queues are an example of distributed systems. These patterns can retrieve architectures that are container-oriented.

The abundant availability of containers capable of implementing interfaces that mount and run allow for easier operation and implementation of a framework for queues. In this way, a developer or programmer is only required to construct containers that are capable of taking input data on filesystems and altering them to another output file. As a result, the container in this instance then becomes a stage of a work queue. For all other work that is required in formulating a work queue, this can be achieved by utilizing a simple queue capable of being reused when required.

The final Kubernetes system pattern examined in this section is the gather/scatter pattern. Within this particular system, a client that's externally operating will deliver requests initially to a "parent" or "root" node. Thereafter, the root will send the request to a broad amount of servers so that they can perform parallel computations. Partial data will be returned by each shard, and the root will then collect all of the data and deliver them into an individual response to the initial request.

# Chapter 6

# Kubernetes Client Libraries & Extensions

Kubernetes Client Libraries tend to operate certain tasks including authentication for users. Many client libraries are able to uncover and utilize the Kubernetes Service Account in order to authenticate whether each API client is operating within a Kubernetes cluster. On the other hand, client libraries are able to comprehend the format for the kubeconfig file in order to read all of the credentials, along with the address for the API Server.

Notably, most client libraries for Kubernetes are under the purview of Kubernetes SIG API machinery. Not to mention, there are also client libraries that are community-maintained. Full lists of the client libraries for the Kubernetes platform can be found on their website: kubernetes.io.

In order to effectively write applications that employ Kubernetes REST API, you are not required to employ API requests and call types on your own. What's more is that you are able to employ a client library for whichever language of programming that you choose to use.

Kubernetes client libraries commonly deal with certain tasks aligned with authentication for users. Now, note that most client libraries are capable of discovering and employing a Kubernetes Service Account for authentication. However, this is only for instances when the API client is operating within a Kubernetes cluster.

One of the fascinating facets of Kubernetes is that you are able to extend the system's API if you wish to construct a platform for leveraging the full expanse of Kubernetes' power.

All of the various mechanisms that are available for employing API extensions are categorized under (CRD) Custom Resource Definition, along with an Aggregated API Server. Moreover, the APIs that use these mechanisms are each able to be accessed through Kubectl—you do not need to use a CLI if you wish to access them.

Mainly, there are 3 primary constructs that are involved in an extended Kubernetes API. These 3 components are as follows:

1. Custom sub-resource

2. Custom controller

3. Custom Kind

Custom Kind is a specific construct facilitating users to clearly define requirements that are domain-specific within a format that is declarative. For instance, a Kind for PostgreSQL that is custom is able to support a declarative model for formulating users and several databases. Indeed, a Custom Kind is analogous to native Kubernetes Kinds such as Service and Pod. Moreover, this will include status, spec, and metadata section.

Custom Controller refers to a Kubernetes controller performing reunification of cluster's state through viewing delete and update events directly onto Kubernetes Kinds within a cluster. Note that this may include native Kinds, such as Service, Pod, and Deployment - all of which were mentioned earlier in this book.

Custom Sub-facilitates uses to define actions that are relatively fine-grained on its Kind; this applies to whether the Kubernetes Kind is custom or native. Devoid of a sub-resource, Kubernetes will afford basic CRUD moves on whichever Kind is chosen. It is very important to consider that not all extended APIs will incorporate all constructs. In truth, 4 patterns have been outlined has it pertains to an extended API. These are as follows:

**Custom Controller + Custom Kind.** As the most well-known pattern, this affords users to utilize a Custom Kind to model one's domain equipment in a declarative manner. This will include the appropriate logic for reconciling testate of a cluster through reacting immediately to the full range of occurrences that relate to the Custom Kind. Operator Pattern is the most popular reference name for this particular pattern.

Notably, this pattern is able to be employed through Aggregated API Servers *and* CRD formats.

The formula of **Custom sub-resource + Custom Kind + Custom Controller** is the same as Operator Pattern. Moreover, it is fully capable of supporting certain custom actions that exist outside of CRUD on each Custom Kind. This is done through the custom sub-resource. If you wish to implement this specific pattern through only the Aggregated API Servers format, the **Custom sub-resource + Custom Controller** is the formula that must be used.

Granted, this will not be able to define an entirely new Kind. Instead, the logic for reconciliation is achieved by the custom controller only on events that are concerned with Kinds registered within a cluster beforehand.

Also, a custom sub-resource is utilized to access data collected by a custom controller. One of the best examples of this is an instance where a controller is responsible for maintaining and collecting data pertaining to the composition of the custom sub-resource and where Kubernetes Objects are utilized to retrieve this data. Importantly, this can only be achieved through employing the Aggregated API Servers.

In a Custom sub-resource, a custom controller is entirely absent. Moreover, this custom sub-resource is most commonly utilized as a mechanism to learn more intensive information pertaining to some facet of Kubernetes Object. The best way to exemplify this is by examining a server for metrics. Moreover, a metrics server is designed to retrieve data from Prometheus and thereafter ensures that it is made widely available through a custom sub-resource. Once again, only the Aggregated API Servers (AA) can implement this particular pattern.

51

It is very important to note that in every wherein an emerging Custom Kind is introduced, this pattern can be referred to an Operator Pattern. In addition, the final two patterns are primarily focused on facilitating the capability to trigger actions that are custom on Kubernetes Objects.

By analyzing all of the currently accessible examples, this section as presented 4 distinct occurrences and patterns that combine all of the constructs available today. When examining API extensions by using extension patterns, the proper mechanisms, tools, and examples are readily at your disposal when you begin formulating the extended API. Kubernetes is highly configurable and extensible. As a result, there is rarely a need to fork or submit patches to the Kubernetes project code.

Even still, there are more aspects to consider when on the subject on Kubernetes extensions. The rest of this chapter will delve deeper into these areas and present a few where the concepts are most applicable to users.

Before delving deeper into Kubernetes Extensions, Configuration is worth your consideration. Flags and files of Configuration are well docents within the section of Reference in the online documentation. Underneath each individual binary, you must consider that files and flags will not be perennially changeable within a Kubernetes service that is hosted—or even a managed distribution installation.

In instances where these are able to be changed, they can usually only be changed by cluster administrators. Not to mention, these will certainly be able to be changed in versions of Kubernetes in the near future. What's more, setting these up will most certainly require a restarting process. For this reason, users are well advised only to use these when options are limited, or if this is the only option available.

Moving back to Kubernetes extensions, it is worth being reminded that extensions are specific components of software responsible for extending and integrating on a deeper level with Kubernetes. Even more, extensions adapt to support and maintain newer forms of system hardware fully.

In most cases, cluster administrators tend to utilize a distribution and to toast instances with regard to Kubernetes. Consequently, many users of Kubernetes will be required to have extensions installed and many users will no longer be required to author brand new extensions.

Specifically designed to automate through writing particular client programs, beneficial automation can be garnered through all programs that write and or read to Kubernetes API. Moreover, there are certain patterns that can write client programs configured to operate effectively with Kubernetes that is called a Controller pattern.

When combining new APIs for Automation, users will often need also to consider adding a control loop that is capable of writing and reading new APIs in the system. When this occurs, this pattern is referred to as an Operator. Also, control loops and Custom APIs are able to be used for controlling resources which includes policies, storage, and other features as well.

When users are extending Kubernetes API through the addition of custom resources, these newly attained resources will collapse into newly formed API Groups within the platform. Interestingly, users are not able to change, alter, or even replace API groups that are already in place. Indeed, the addition of an API will not allow users to directly influence existing API behavior, such as Pods, for instance. However, users will be able to do this through API Access Extensions.

Whenever a formal request manages to reach the Kubernetes API Server, the sequence is as follows: First, it will be authenticated, followed by being Authorized. Thereafter, the steps are entirely subject to a range of versions of Admission Control. All of the steps in this process affords extensions points.

Kubernetes also has a bevy of methods for authentication that are built right into the platform. Also, it is able to be placed behind a proxy for authentication.

Another area worth examining with regard to Kubernetes Extensions are the Infrastructure Extensions. Notably, there are two key forms of Infrastructure Extensions. First, Storage Plugins: to set volume types devoid of support that is built-in, Flex Volumes are required. This happens by through having a Kubelet call directly for a Binary Plugin for effectively mounting the volume.

Next, Device Plugins: these afford nodes across the platform to find new resources for Nodes through a particular Device Plugin.

## Scheduler Extensions

This is specifically a form of controller responsible for keeping close watch over pods, thereby assigning pods to nodes as well. Moreover, the scheduler default can be entirely replaced, even as still uses other components of the Kubernetes platform. Additionally, a few schedulers are able to operate simultaneously.

This is particularly significant when considering that all users of Kubernetes are not required to significantly alter the scheduler within the platform in any way whatsoever. Not to mention, the schedulers are also capable of fully supporting a webhook. This allows for a backend webhook, otherwise known as a scheduler extension, to effectively prioritize and filter all nodes that are selected for each pod.

There are myriad benefits to API Extensions within the Kubernetes platform. For instance, at the Platform layer, implementing a system will introduce all new abstractions for delivering whichever platform that the user desires. There used only to be a single avenue through which new abstractions were produced- this was through wrapping all of the APIs of the layer underneath.

Kubernetes extensions can be written as platform abstractions rather than API wrappers. Thus, this results in a few advantages:

1. Tools that are written specifically for Kubernetes base, such as Helm, are very easily utilized with certain abstractions that are uniquely produced as API extensions. However, this is likely

not to be the case with regard to abstractions that are produced specifically as wrappers for API.

2. End users of Kubernetes' abstractions are not required to adopt new CLI in order to consume them fully.

3. To achieve maximum simplicity, sometimes abstractions that are produced as API wrappers can shield many of the underlying functions of API. As a result, end users are far less likely to acquire the level of control that is needed.

4. Auditing and other forms of advanced functionality that can work effectively with the base format of Kubernetes are able to very easily be leveraged for certain abstractions that are produced by only using API extensions. However, this is likely not to be the case when considering abstractions as strictly API wrappers. Thus, users will be required to care for certain advanced functions for abstraction layers within the code.

# Conclusion

Thank you again for purchasing this book! I hope this book was able to help you understand how to operate Kubernetes in its full capacity while providing in-depth information about the platform overall.

The next step is to begin implementing the strategies and practical methods presented within this text. If you are looking for new ways to use this platform or are simply trying to acquire more information about Kubernetes, this is the perfect text for you!

Given the abundance of information available on the Internet pertaining to best practices of digital platforms, there has yet to be any extensive text on the Kubernetes platform. With 6 chapters that present and elaborate on the multiple features of Kubernetes, you are now fully equipped to maximize this platform for everything that it is.

Be sure to study all of the examples presented to ensure the smoothest operation and navigation of the platform. This will save you time and energy while making sure that you get the most out of your projects.

Finally, if you enjoyed this book, then I'd like to ask you for a favor: would you be kind enough to leave a review for this book on Amazon? It'd be greatly appreciated!

Thank you and good luck!

Made in the USA
Middletown, DE
01 November 2020